To:

From:

Praise for
THE LEADERSHIP SECRETS
OF SANTA CLAUS

"I've always loved Santa Claus—and now that I know his leadership secrets, I love him even more! Read this book and learn how returning to your childhood can make you a better adult—and a better leader."

—**KEN BLANCHARD**, *New York Times*
bestselling author of *The One Minute Manager*

"This warm, wonderful book is loaded with great ideas for leaders at all levels to build a peak performing team of highly motivated people."

—**BRIAN TRACY**, *New York Times*
bestselling author, speaker

"*The Leadership Secrets of Santa Claus* will have your workshop running smoother, your elves happier, and your business thriving, not just during the holidays, but all year long. I think it's destined to be a classic for years to come!"

—**VIC CONANT**, CEO of Nightingale-Conant Corporation

"Forget the naughty. *The Leadership Secrets of Santa Claus* makes the nicest gift for any leader in your life—not just at Christmastime, but all year long! It offers a creative twist on some sage business advice that too often gets forgotten. If you want a reward for being good—*this is it!*"

—**DR. BOB NELSON**, bestselling author
of *1501 Ways to Reward Employees*

"*The Leadership Secrets of Santa Claus* delivers classic leadership lessons in an entertaining style. With the best lessons on how to keep your business running smoothly all year round, this book is a must-read for every leader, at any time of year."

—**STEDMAN GRAHAM**, bestselling author,
speaker, entrepreneur

"This is a brilliant book with solid substance on transformational leadership. A great read."

—**NIDO QUBEIN**, president of High Point University,
chairman of Great Harvest Bread Co.

"*The Leadership Secrets of Santa Claus* is a rare gem. It's filled with tools that any leader can put in effect TODAY to change the productivity and effectiveness of their own workplace, but it's told in such an engaging way that you won't want to put it down."

—**ANDY ANDREWS**, *New York Times* bestselling
author of *The Noticer* and *The Traveler's Gift*

Photo Credits: Cover image © Joe_Potato/Getty Images
Internals: page vii, © fotohunter/Shutterstock; page viii, xiv, 16, 30, 44, 56, 68, 82, 96, 110, 126, 140, © nadianb/Shutterstock; page x, © Christopher Elwell/Shutterstock; page 2, © Vicki L. Miller/Shutterstock; page 4, 36, 52, 88, 92, 98, 118, 128, 130, 142, © Milles Studio/Shutterstock; page 8, © stefanphotozemun/Shutterstock; page 10, © Ryan Jorgensen - Jorgo/Shutterstock; page 13, 132, © Myvisuals/Shutterstock; page 14, © inhauscreative/iStock; page 18, © mis1il/Shutterstock; page 22, © Vladimir Melnikov/iStock; page 25, © BlueOrange Studio/Shutterstock; page 27, © lola1960/Shutterstock; page 28, © K. Jensen/Shutterstock; page 32, © Julia Sudnitskaya/Shutterstock; page 34, © Tatyana Domnicheva/Shutterstock; page 40, © HASLOO/iStock; page 46, 78, © gpointstudio/Shutterstock; page 48, © FamVeld/Shutterstock; page 50, © evgenyatamanenko/iStock; page 55, © cynoclub/Shutterstock; page 58, © Ricardo Reitmeyer/Shutterstock; page 61, © Nickolya/Shutterstock; page 64, © Yuganov Konstantin/Shutterstock; page 66, © Thanakrit Sathavornmanee/Shutterstock; page 70, © Subbotina Anna/Shutterstock; page 76, © LineWeight/Shutterstock; page 74, © Derek Hatfield/Shutterstock; page 87, © Sugarless/Shutterstock; page 90, © Stanislav Vinogradov/Shutterstock; page 100, © Vitalina Rybakova/Shutterstock; page 103, © marekuliasz/Shutterstock; page 104, © sarsmis/Shutterstock; page 106, © Kevin Lepp/Shutterstock; page 112, © Sean Locke Photography/Shutterstock; page 115, © Evgeny Atamanenko/Shutterstock; page 117, © Smileus/Shutterstock; page 122, © Evgeny Karandaev/Shutterstock; page 124, © giggsy25/Shutterstock; page 137, © udra11/Shutterstock

Published by Simple Truths, an imprint of Sourcebooks, Inc.
P.O. Box 4410, Naperville, Illinois 60567-4410
(630) 961-3900 • Fax: (630) 961-2168 • sourcebooks.com

Originally published in 2003 in the United States of America by Performance Systems Corporation.

Printed and bound in China.
OGP 10 9 8 7 6 5 4 3 2 1

THE
LEADERSHIP SECRETS of SANTA CLAUS

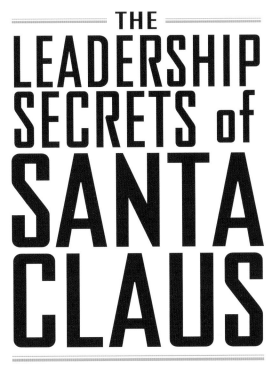

ERIC HARVEY

simple **truths**
▶ Small books. **BIG IMPACT.**

IGNITE READS
spark impact in just one hour

A SACKFUL OF CONTENTS

Santa's Helpers...ix

Introduction..xi

1. Build a Wonderful Workshop 1

2. Choose Your Reindeer Wisely 17

3. Make a List and Check It Twice 31

4. Listen to the Elves 45

5. Say Ho Ho Ho, but Don't Forget the Snow ... 57

6. Give Them Gifts That Last a Lifetime 69

7. Get Beyond the Red Wagons 83

8. Share the Milk and Cookies 97

9. Find Out Who's Naughty and Nice 111

10. Be Good for Goodness Sake 127

Closing Thoughts 141

About the Author 145

SANTA'S HELPERS

David Cottrell and **Al Lucia** have helped hundreds of organizations and their leaders build high-performance workplaces with motivated coworkers. Their work is based on the belief that effective leaders accomplish "big things" by **giving** employees clear goals, solid accountabilities, and ongoing feedback, coaching, and recognition. These are the leadership traits of the Santa Claus in each of us.

Special thanks to our creative "head elf" **Steve Ventura** for helping us get this big thing done.

It's Not Easy Being
Santa Claus!

Give people exactly what they want, and Ho, Ho, Ho—everybody loves good Ol' Santa. But miss one or two items on the list—or forget to include the batteries—and you'd better be ready for the alligator tears, the fat jokes, the stupid songs, the withheld cookies, the wet laps, the yanks on the beard, and the "I could do Santa's job better than Santa" remarks. And that's only half of why it's not **EASY** being me!

There's no doubt that my biggest challenges come from two roles that people rarely associate with this red-cheeked, bag-carrying sleigh driver: Santa the **MANAGER** and Santa the **LEADER**.

I am, after all, running a business here. I'm a boss. I've got responsibilities—both to the gift-*getters* and the gift-*makers*. There are workers to lead, letters to read, orders to fill, processes to manage, things to buy, things to make, standards to maintain, new technologies to adopt, skills to develop, elf problems to solve, and reindeer droppings to scoop (although I delegate that one). Trust me, I've got some big boots to fill.

Think your job is tough? *You* try recruiting in, and for, the North Pole; *you* try retooling your plant—and retraining your people—every year to produce the newest fads in toys; *you* try delivering tons of presents on a route as big as mine—all in one night.

No, it's not easy being Santa Claus. But in spite of that, **I love what I do.** People need me—they depend on me. We're doing something important here. And knowing that gives me the energy to carry the sack, lead the pack, and keep coming back.

By now, you may be wondering how I meet all of these challenges and responsibilities—how I manage to bring everyone and everything together to complete our mission. Some people think I use magic. But really, there's no magic about it.

So, if it's not magic, then what *is* my secret? I actually have ten—ten practical strategies for leading others and getting big things done all year long. They're called the "Leadership Secrets of Santa Claus," and I'm here to share them with *you*.

They are my gifts to you. And I guarantee that if you apply them, you'll find these "secrets" more valuable than anything you might have written on your holiday wish list.

READ ON! LEAD ON!

Santa Claus

Santa Claus

BUILD A WONDERFUL
WORKSHOP

Make the Mission the Main Thing

What's your vision of my workplace? Do you see candy canes and chestnuts? Whistling and singing? Busy little elves and reindeer with smiles on their faces scurrying around to make and package toys? If so, your image is right on—except for the candy canes and chestnuts.

Yes, we do run a productive and happy place here. And that's in spite of the intense pressures and challenges we face—ones that undoubtedly were *not* included in your vision of us. So how do we do it? Just how do *I* keep everyone, including myself, on

track and motivated throughout each year—all for one long night's big splash? The answer is simple: through an unwavering and uncompromising focus on **OUR MISSION**. And as the leader, I've taken several steps to establish and maintain that focus.

First, I've made sure that all the elves and reindeer

know what our mission is ("Making spirits bright by building and delivering high-quality toys to good little girls and boys") and why it's important.

Second, I've spent time with individual employees—discussing how their respective jobs specifically link with and contribute to the accomplishment of our mission.

Third, I've kept the mission "in front of folks" by posting it on walls, discussing it at staff meetings and training sessions, including it in internal correspondence, and a host of other activities that help ensure it stays our central focal point.

Finally, I've made it a core component of our decision-making and work-planning processes. If an action we're considering doesn't support our mission either directly or indirectly, we don't do it!

With all the team members we have, orders we get, toys we make, and issues we face, it could be way too easy to dilute ourselves, head off on tangents, or just plain lose sight of why we're here. We avoid those distractions by keeping our mission at the heart of everything we do—by making our mission our main thing. I recommend that you do the same in *your* workshop!

Focus on Your People as Well as Your Purpose

Here's a nugget of leadership wisdom that I've picked up over the decades—something you can take to one of the toy banks we occasionally deliver: you can't possibly focus on your mission without also focusing on the folks that make your mission happen. And besides, since you manage **THINGS** and lead **PEOPLE**, common sense suggests that it's *people* who are at the core of all leadership activities.

But alas, common sense apparently isn't all that common. There is a handful of managers out there who don't get it—they don't get the message, and they don't get the positive results that the message can help produce. That point was clearly brought home by a short letter I received several years ago:

Dear Santa:

This year I only want one thing—a manager who cares as much about me as the work I'm doing. It's hard to be committed when there's no reciprocation. Please help!

Now that's a sad commentary...and a tall order to fill. There was no need to check our production schedule. I already knew that "caring leaders" weren't on our list of deliverables. But I needed to respond in some way, so I decided to do two things: 1) Write this book, and 2) Vow to do my very best never to be the kind of leader described in that letter.

7

I'm happy (even jolly) to say I've done both. Writing this book was by far the easier of the two responses; living up to my vow—turning my good intentions into predictable behaviors—was more challenging. It took abandoning a few old behaviors and adopting a few new ones; it required commitment, self-discipline, concentration, and prioritization. And I needed to monitor my progress (and still do), through both self-evaluation and periodic feedback from the workshop team, by providing answers to the following:

In the last several months, what have I done to:

 Be accessible (physically and mentally) to employees who would like my attention?

 Provide employees with the training, tools, resources, and feedback required for success?

 Help team members maintain an appropriate balance between their professional and personal lives?

 Demonstrate respect for employees' time and talents as well as respect for them as individuals?

These, and many others like them, are the questions I ask—and the things I do—to make sure I focus on

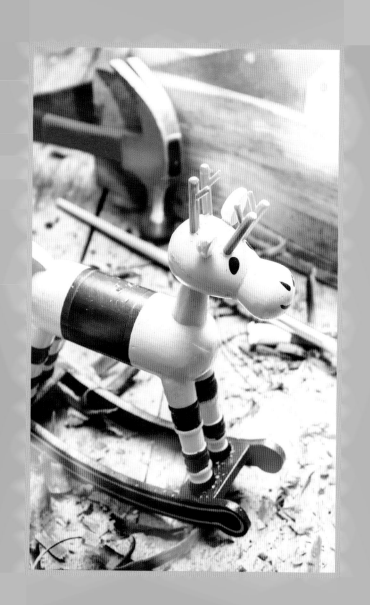

the wonderful workers who comprise our wonderful workshop. What questions do *you* ask? What action items would I find on *your* list?

Let Values Be Your Guide

It was a Tuesday morning, and I was conducting a leadership development training session in the workshop classroom. I gave each participant a set of plastic building blocks along with an assignment: "Build a model of a wonderful workshop." The purpose of the task was twofold:

 1. **Test student creativity and thinking, and**

 2. **Provide me with ideas for improving our North Pole facility.**

After starting the exercise, I left the room.

After some time had passed, I returned to the room

to conclude the exercise. As I moved from table to table, I was truly impressed by the array of detailed models with structural components like smokestacks, loading ramps, conveyor belts, sleigh landing pads, cafeterias, gyms, offices, and even high-tech classrooms.

When I came to Virginia's model, however, I was taken aback. There, in front of her, were six vertical columns—and nothing more. "Need more time?" I asked. "No thanks," she answered. "I'm done." Hearing that, I probed further: "Virginia, I'm not sure I understand. All the other models are very detailed structures, but all you have are six columns. No walls, no roof, no nothing. How come?" The explanation she offered is where you'll find the lesson for leaders everywhere:

"Well, Santa, it seems to me that what makes a workshop wonderful is not walls and ceilings, but what happens *inside* those walls and *under* those ceilings. It's not how a workshop *stands*, but what it *stands for* that makes it special. These six columns you see are pillars, and they represent values—the values of respect, integrity, quality, customer service, responsibility, and teamwork. I found them listed on our website. Maybe for some folks they're just words, but for me they're blueprints to follow. And that's where leadership comes in. **Making sure that everyone knows what values are important** and then **helping everyone turn those good beliefs into everyday behaviors** is how leaders create a great place to work. At least that's how I see it. And that's why my model looks the way it does. Did

I do okay?"

With a huge grin on my face and a twinkle in my eye, I responded, "Yes, Virginia. That *is* a wonderful workshop. And I think that you are going to be a wonderful leader. Thank you for giving me such a valuable gift."

SANTA SUMMARY:
BUILD A WONDERFUL WORKSHOP

✓ **Make the Mission the Main Thing**

✓ **Focus on Your People as Well as Your Purpose**

✓ **Let Values Be Your Guide**

CHOOSE YOUR
REINDEER WISELY

Hire Tough So
You Can Manage Easy

You know Dasher and Dancer, Prancer and Vixen; Comet and Cupid, Donner and Blitzen. But do you recall the *least* famous reindeer of all, Misfit? Probably not. He's not here anymore. Unfortunately, I had to let him go decades ago. But I certainly learned a lot from the whole Misfit experience.

It all started when I was faced with hiring a new reindeer to fill a vacant position. Now, I know that pulling the sleigh is a very important job. Ask the reindeer—they'll tell you. But I was busy—very busy. Recruiting and hiring a new puller was just one of the scores of things on my cookie platter. And besides, bringing on new staff can be tedious, bureaucratic, and tiring work. It's not what makes me jolly. So I took the easy route. I did a cursory résumé review, conducted a quick, pro forma interview, and grabbed the first warm antlered-body that appeared halfway decent.

Misfit was appropriately named all right. After a short period of putting his best hoof forward, the problems began. He'd show up late and then display a less-than-desirable attitude when I called him on it. More and more, he'd carry less and less of his share of the load. That made the sleigh pull to the right—forcing the left-side crew to work harder in order for us to stay straight. The harder they worked, the more irritated they became, and the harder it was for me to keep the reins in check.

I ended up spending way too much time watching Misfit, re-re-retraining him, counseling him, and handling complaints about him from the other reindeer—and the elves as well. Pretty soon, he was bringing the whole team down, and productivity was going down with them. All of that because of one Misfit reindeer…all of that because I cut corners and allowed joining the team to be way too easy.

That was then. Now I do things much differently. Through the Misfit experience, I've come to realize that:

1. **Because it's employees who ultimately make our mission happen, staffing is my single most important responsibility.**

2. **The time I spend hiring the right way is nothing compared to the time I'll *have* to spend dealing with the wrong reindeer.**

Take a hiring lesson from Santa. Invest in doing it right up front and everyone—especially you—will be happier down the road.

Promote the Right Ones...
for the Right Reasons

Just listen to his cute little song (go ahead…sing it to yourself) and you'll quickly realize that Rudolph wasn't always the lead reindeer. In fact, he didn't get that promotion until one foggy night about a century ago. Before that, Donner had the top spot; Donner was "the deer." And as it turned out, promoting Donner was **THE PROBLEM**.

Now, don't get me wrong. Donner was not a bad reindeer. He was a great reindeer! One of the best pullers I've ever had. He was strong, fast, and dependable. Donner was a pro—as a puller. So when it came time to promote a new lead, he was my obvious choice. He had earned it. And I assumed that the best puller would make the best leader. Well, to quote another old song title, "it ain't necessarily so."

To say that Donner had a difficult time is an understatement. The lead job was different than the puller job—with skill and ability requirements that I hadn't tested for and that he couldn't meet.

He was in over his head, and he was miserable. So were the other reindeer…and so was I. Donner needed to go back to the job he was good at, and a new lead— the right lead—needed to be found.

Rudolph was a decent puller, but by no means was he the strongest or fastest of the crew. When he first joined the team, some of the other reindeer laughed, called him names, and excluded him from their games. They're not an easy bunch to "bond" with. But that changed as they (and I) began to notice that there was something special about Rudolph; he seemed to have a knack for getting things done with others…a *nose* for leadership. So I decided to consider him for the lead.

This time, I started to take some notes. I created two columns: 1) The tasks, duties, and responsibilities of the lead position, and 2) The characteristics, talents, values, abilities, and attitudes that I felt were necessary to perform those tasks successfully—and to support our overall mission. Then I tested Rudolph and the other candidates against those criteria. He was a standout. He had "the right stuff."

So, on that foggy night long ago, Rudolph got his shot. And the rest, as they say, is history. It's a *wonderful* history…and an unforgettable lesson.

Go for the Diversity Advantage

It used to be that our elves were pretty much all alike— same size, same pointed ears, same little green suits,

same way of talking...same everything. Whenever we needed new elves, I automatically looked for and brought on workers that fit the standard mold. Why not? That's the way it was for years and years—and it seemed to be working just fine. We rarely messed up an order and we had never missed our December 24 delivery. I was one happy sleigh driver—that is, until two things happened.

First, I found out that we had competitors. Department stores, online retailers, discount chains, and a whole host of other manufacturers and toy distributors were moving in on the market we had cornered for decades. They had all kinds of workers (not just elves), and they were gaining ground on our operation.

I wasn't sure how to address the challenge of competition, but I knew that *something* needed to be done. Staying with "business as usual" probably wouldn't serve us well that much longer.

Soon after discovering that we had competition, the second thing happened: a group of North Pole

politicians passed a law that said we had to expand our hiring practices; we had to start bringing on different kinds of toy makers—not just the little pointy-eared fellas we'd been employing forever.

It wasn't easy, but we did it. We did it **ALL**. And in the process, we got more than a Santa's sackful of

unexpected benefits. It didn't take long to discover that our "different" toy makers came bearing gifts. They brought new skills, perspectives, and ideas to the workshop. They gave us more than one way of thinking, planning, producing, and problem solving. They made us better, stronger, and much more in touch with the different shapes, sizes, and colors of customers that we serve. And all that has helped us more than hold our own with all those competing Santa wannabes out there.

What started out as a challenging situation—to merely comply with a requirement—has become our most significant competitive advantage. And it can be yours as well. Believe Santa Claus; believe in diversity.

SANTA SUMMARY:
CHOOSE YOUR REINDEER WISELY

✓ **Hire Tough So You Can Manage Easy**

✓ **Promote the Right Ones...for the Right Reasons**

✓ **Go for the Diversity Advantage**

3

MAKE A LIST
AND CHECK IT TWICE

To Do List

Plan Your Work

Respond to endless streams of request letters, make millions of high-quality products—according to exact specifications—364 days a year, package toys so they arrive in perfect condition, and deliver the exact right gift to the exact right person in the exact right house millions of times in one single night. That's what we do every year. We do it flawlessly, and none of it happens by accident!

We begin by breaking down our one huge annual goal (our mission) of "delivering the goods" into a series of manageable, bite-size subgoals. We have them

for the shop in general, the teams within the shop, and individuals within the teams.

Whether in direct production and delivery, or a "behind the scenes" support function, **EVERYONE** has goals—including me. Our goals are specific yet flexible—allowing for changing conditions and circumstances. And because staff "buy-in" and commitment are so important to achieving our objectives, I make sure that *everyone* has input in the goal-setting process.

Once our individual and group goals are identified, we move into the planning (making "the list") phase. Plans provide us with the direction, focus, and organization we need to stay on task. And since none of us here at the Pole have perfect memories, we make sure they're *written* action plans.

We develop our plans by answering six questions for each set goal:

1. **WHAT needs to be accomplished?**

2. **WHY does it need to be done? (How does it contribute to our overall mission?)**

3. **WHEN does it need to be accomplished?**

4. **WHERE am I/are we now in relation to this goal?**

5. **WHO will be involved in accomplishing this?**

6. **HOW will it be accomplished? (What specific steps and activities are involved, and what resources are required?)**

After answering these questions with as much detail as possible, we perform the last of the planning activities: adding contingencies. We do our best to anticipate the unexpected by asking "but what if..." questions. *But what if the snowfall is way above or below normal this year? But what if a flu bug works its way through the shop during peak production time? But what if*

the computer with our delivery address book crashes? Certainly we can't predict all the obstacles we may face, but combining some thought with past experiences does enhance our readiness to deal with Murphy's Law.

Work Your Plan

None of us here at the workshop are particularly fond of negative surprises—especially me. They take the twinkle right out of my eyes. Fact is, we face enough challenges already without manufacturing any more on our own. So we don't wait until estimated completion dates to see if we've reached our goals. Once we make our list (plan), we check it twice. Actually, we check it a lot *more* than twice.

We schedule (as in, set specific times on our calendars) frequent progress checks as part of the work-planning process. I meet with teams and individuals—and they meet amongst themselves, without me—to measure the status of our goals against predetermined progress "benchmarks." At those meetings, we ask the following:

 Is each goal still valid and doable?

 Are we where we should be in terms of attaining each goal?

 Have any conditions or circumstances changed since we originally set each goal?

 Do we need to make any changes to our goals, our action plans, or our performance levels?

The answers to these questions provide the intelligence we need to guide us in bringing our important mission to life.

As the sign on our workshop wall says:

> *If We Want to Hear Jingle Bells Ringing on the 24th, We Need to Set and Live by Goals...All Year Long!*

Make the Most of What You Have

There's another sign hanging in our workshop. It reads:

So Many Toys, So Little Time

It serves as a reminder for us (and a clue for you) about

overcoming big challenges and accomplishing big goals: you have to maximize the resources available to you.

Goal setting—planning your work and then working your plan—not only leads to effectiveness, it also fosters efficiency: it helps you minimize waste. And if there's one thing we hate around here, it's waste. Considering the volume of orders and deliveries we deal with annually, we'd quickly go out of business if we didn't make the absolute best use of our resources: time, money, materials, and the talents of our elves and reindeer.

Because resources are so important to us, we've gone well beyond merely relying on goal action plans to ensure efficiency. The best example of this is a workshop-wide team we created called "Waste Watchers" (no connection to my "bowl full of jelly" belly!). The sole purpose of the group is to identify and eliminate inefficient or wasteful business practices. The following presents just a few of the strategies they've come up with to help us do more with less.

MAKING THE MOST OF TIME

❋ Prioritize tasks (do the most important things first) and use "to do" lists to organize daily activities.

❋ Start and end meetings promptly—and issue agendas in advance.

❋ Teach time-management skills and techniques.

❋ Take advantage of timesaving technology.

MAKING THE MOST OF MONEY

❋ Buy in discounted bulk whenever appropriate.

❋ Shop for the best prices on materials, supplies, equipment, and services.

❋ Communicate electronically to reduce long-distance charges.

❋ Think pennies as well as dollars—a few cents saved here and there add up quickly.

MAKING THE MOST OF MATERIALS AND EQUIPMENT

❋ "Measure twice, cut once."

❋ Reuse and recycle whenever possible.

❋ Be religious about preventative maintenance.

❋ Invest in extended warranties.

MAKING THE MOST OF EMPLOYEE TALENT AND EXPERTISE

* ❄ Involve the *people* with the *knowledge* in the *decisions.*
* ❄ Match jobs with worker skills and interests.
* ❄ Enhance employee expertise through training and developmental assignments.
* ❄ Encourage employees to share their knowledge with others.

SANTA SUMMARY:
MAKE A LIST AND CHECK IT TWICE

☑ **Plan Your Work**

☑ **Work Your Plan**

☑ **Make the Most of What You Have**

4

LISTEN
TO THE ELVES

Open Your Ears to Participation

Way, way back when we started in this business, there were a lot less orders to fill and a lot fewer houses to visit. We didn't have even 10 percent of the staff we have now, and I did quite a bit of the toy making myself. In fact, I did quite a bit of *everything* myself. But eventually, as our operation grew in size and complexity, it became necessary to move away from **DOING** (except for my big deliveries) and devote my time to **MANAGING**. The good news was that I had a wealth of experience to call upon as a manager. The bad news: I used that experience…to a fault.

Because I had "been there," I was pretty sure I knew more than—or at least as much as—the elves did about toy production. When a decision needed to be made, it was me alone who made it; when a process needed to be modified or upgraded, I devised the plan; when new equipment needed to be selected...well, you get the picture. Running the show was my job. Besides, who else could make those calls? Certainly not the elves. They had neither the experience for, nor the interest in, administrative work like that. Or so I thought. Until, that is, one day when out in the workshop there arose such a clatter I sprang from my office to see what was the matter.

It turns out the gears of the toy production line had grinded to an unexpected halt. The inspection process that I had just implemented (after two weeks of closed-door design) was slowing things to a snail's pace. The elves were going crazy trying to keep up with the production schedule. And then the new mechanical assembler that I researched and purchased let loose with a strange thumping noise, coughed up a billow of smoke, and shut down completely.

A quick investigation revealed that my new procedure and the assembly machine were both flawed. "We could have told you," said one of the elves, "if you just had asked us in the beginning…and really **LISTENED** to what we had to say." I responded, "So what can we do to get things going again?" With that, a bunch of them huddled for a little while and came up with a better inspection process—and some modifications that got the assembler up and running again. We were

back in business; the elves were patting each other on the back and smiling. And I had come to realize that involving workers in running the operation—and in making decisions that affect them—is a key strategy for leadership success.

Now I ask for (and listen to) the elves' ideas and opinions on most everything we do. I even let *them* make many of the toy-making decisions we face. And the production line has never run better.

Pay Attention to How You're Perceived

As our challenges have grown with each new season, more and more I rely on teamwork, collaboration, and the contributions of each member of the workshop team. Ensuring that those things happen requires effective leadership on my part, and I began to wonder how I was doing on that front. The only way to find out was to ask…and then listen.

I began doing employee attitude surveys and conducting focus groups. I even established a "North Pole feedback hotline" to help find out what everyone thought about me as a leader and to provide a vehicle for collecting input on how I could improve.

So I listened…and I acted. I do to this very day. And I'm a much better Santa because of it. I pay attention to what my elves (and others) feel. Perceptions are realities for those that hold them, and I must deal with those realities in order to lead effectively. And so too must you.

Whether it's through formal surveys, hotlines, informal discussions, "slip me an anonymous note about my leadership" invitations, or whatever makes the most sense for your business, you must find your own way to **ASK**, **LISTEN**, and **ACT**.

Walk Awhile in *Their* Shoes

My most cherished gift of all occupies a place of prominence on a bookshelf in my office: a pair of small felt elf shoes (the kind with pointed toes that curl up). I received them several years ago. They just appeared on my desk one day, along with a "Dear Santa" letter.

Now, this letter was much different than the kind I'm used to reading. It didn't ask for anything. It was a thank-you letter. I consider it a written commendation. And with great pride, I offer it as your next leadership lesson:

Dear Santa,

Thank you for being such a great boss. We know it isn't easy being you—with all the pressures and responsibilities that you have. We also know that we're not always the easiest bunch to deal with. But with all that you have going on, and with all that we sometimes throw your way, you still manage to remain considerate and understanding. You show us, by your behaviors, that you realize it's challenging for all of us in the workshop too. That makes us appreciate you even more.

Thank you, Santa, for making the effort to see things through our eyes and for walking in these smaller, yet nonetheless important, shoes. While you may not literally be in our shoes, you heart most certainly is.

The Elves

SANTA SUMMARY:
LISTEN TO THE ELVES

☑ **Open Your Ears to Participation**

☑ **Pay Attention to How You're Perceived**

☑ **Walk Awhile in Their Shoes**

5

SAY HO HO HO, BUT DON'T FORGET THE SNOW

Build Contagious
Enthusiasm

To truly build a workshop that is filled with positive energy, I not only need to set the example individually, but also make the goal of recognizing positive performance part of **EVERY** reindeer and elf's job expectations. And that's just what I've done—along with establishing a set of guidelines ("Santa's Recognition Rules") for everyone to follow in order to provide effective, high-quality recognition.

SANTA'S RECOGNITION RULES

 Make It Timely

Give recognition as soon as possible. Don't wait until later, because sometimes "later" never comes.

 Get Specific

Tell recognition recipients exactly what they did that was positive. A mere "Good job, Rudolph" really doesn't say that much.

 Be Appreciative

Tell team members what their positive performance means to you, to the other elves and reindeer, and to the goals of the workshop—and thank them for that.

 Get Personal

Adjust the style and method of your recognition to the receiver. Think "different strokes for different folks."

Make It Proportional

Match the type and amount of recognition with the value and impact of the achievement.

Expect the Unexpected

All the positive workplace energy you can create cannot help you totally avoid the inevitable obstacles to workshop success. For example, at the North Pole, we have snow. **LOTS** of snow! But last year, we had

a **MEGA** snowfall—one some called "a thousand-year blizzard." So the morning before the Big Delivery, we got the workshop and sleigh teams together to talk about this challenge and how we might solve the problem.

The first hoof raised and voice we heard came from "Donner the Downer," claiming that the snow was way too high and that this obstacle was unsolvable. He then suggested that we needed to move our delivery date to sometime in January. *Hmmm.* I bit my tongue and waited for the room's response. Suddenly, dozens of waving hands and hooves were raised as team members began to try to outshout each other. One of those hands belonged to little Larry from the Stuffed Toy Section.

After being called on and given the floor, Larry talked about all the people who were counting on our on-time delivery—and how "delaying our deliveries is just not an option." And then, pointing to a series of signs we had posted around the workshop, he asked,

"Don't you remember these?"

 It's the Things That You Least Expect That Hit You the Hardest

 Life's Not Always Fair, So Build a Bridge and Get over It!

 If It Was Easy, Anyone Could Do It!

 Problems Are Opportunities in Disguise!

 There Are Always Solutions!

 Do It Now Because Sometimes "Later" Can Easily Become "Never."

 Complaining Doesn't Solve Problems, Doing Does!

Get Problems Solved...
Together

Because we had such a positive "make it happen" workplace culture, everyone wanted to view this unexpected event as a challenge that we—with some creative thinking—could solve together. So clearly we **HAD** to find a solution. As all this was playing out, I was watching Donner's expression change from sad to supportive. In fact, he was the first one to begin offering possible solutions to our unexpected dilemma. Other team members began to chime in. One idea led to another and another. Bewilderment had quickly become excitement. And a music-to-my-ears chant started and increased in intensity: "We can do this. We can do this. **WE** can do this!"

Contagious enthusiasm was rearing its *beautiful* head!

As a result of our challenge, a team of warehouse elves suggested—and then rigged up—a supersized snowplough to clear the landing strip behind the shop. The backup reindeer volunteered to make up a sleigh team of sixteen for the stormy evening takeoff. We added an aerodynamic "roof rack" device to the back of the sleigh so we could double our cargo load of presents. Rudolph—working with Gilda, our IT elf—installed the latest GPS system to help guide the team through the treacherous storm. **WOW**!

The beauty of this experience was that while it all was happening, I was saying **NOTHING**. I didn't have to because everyone understood the severity of the dilemma, the importance of our mission, and the necessity of being fully committed to finding solutions—together! I just helped everyone get whatever they needed, offered advice and suggestions when asked, got out of the way, and assumed that all-important role of *Santa the Cheerleader*.

My lesson here is that "Ho Ho Ho's" are great for immediate effects, but even more importantly, they're vital for establishing a workshop culture that is built on pride, professionalism, and individual commitment.

SANTA SUMMARY
SAY HO HO HO, BUT DON'T FORGET THE SNOW

✓ **Build Contagious Enthusiasm**

✓ **Expect the Unexpected**

✓ **Get Problems Solved...Together**

6

GIVE THEM GIFTS THAT LAST A LIFETIME

Teach Success Skills

It was several years ago, but I remember it like it was yesterday. That's when I learned an invaluable lesson in leadership from Ian—a candidate who would end up being selected as my EICOT ("Elf in Charge of Training").

During the interview, Ian reversed roles and asked *me* a question: "Santa, what do you see as the purpose of training here at the workshop?" "That's easy," I replied, "It's to teach all of our team members how to do their jobs."

"Well, Santa, the way I see it," answered Ian,

"developing our team is about more than just teaching folks how to do their jobs; it's also about teaching them how to be *successful*. And there is a difference between those two concepts.

"To be sure," Ian continued, "we have to make sure that team members have the knowledge and skills necessary to do their jobs well. Elves must know things like how to make toys and load the sleigh properly. Reindeer must be skilled at pulling that sleigh through take-offs, landings, and long-night flights. And then there's the others—the bookkeepers, the sleigh mechanics, the kitchen staff, the laundry department, etc., etc., etc. Everyone here at the Pole has a job to do and we all must know how to perform our assigned functions with the highest level of quality. But it seems to me that in order to be truly successful, we all need more than just the technical skills of our job classifications."

To clarify his point, Ian asked me a series of questions:

Is an elf really successful if he or she makes good toys but doesn't get along well with others and communicates poorly?

 Is a reindeer really successful if he or she pulls hard but isn't a team player who helps others succeed?

 Are any of us truly successful if we're good at our crafts but display negative attitudes or fail to solve problems effectively?

I didn't have to think long or hard to answer those queries: "No," "No," and "**NO**!"

As a result of that one meeting, Ian got the training job…and I got a valuable lesson.

As the sign on Ian's office wall says:

> *Don't just teach them how to do their jobs. Also teach them how to be SUCCESSFUL!*

Reinforce Relationships

'Twas a month before our big night, when all through the North Pole I assumed elves were busy—every last single soul. I reviewed children's letters—a whole pile on my lap. And then I was ready for a well-deserved nap. When out in the shop there arose such a clatter, I sprang from my chair to see what was the matter. And what to my wondering eyes should appear: two elves going at it with some upset reindeer!

THIS WAS NOT GOOD! Not only had the "combatants" stopped working, but their friction had a negative spill-over effect on the other workers—causing production to slow to a snail's pace. Now I've learned, through experience, that:

1. **Occasional squabbles between workers are inevitable.**

2. **Most workers need help resolving those squabbles.**

3. **It's my job, as their leader, to help them repair what's broken.**

So I called the involved parties up to my office for one of my "Santa intervention" chats. The first

Naughty | Nice

Naughty:
Lynn
Mark
Sara
Emily
Jake
Carter
Johnny

Nice:
Abigail
Noah
Evelyn
Jack
Ava
Emma
Robert
Andrew
Sophia
Carter
Luke

thing I did was to share my observations of what had happened—emphasizing how their coworkers and productivity were negatively impacted. After explaining the problem, I told them how valuable they were to me—and how important it was that they work well together in order for us to accomplish our truly important mission. Next, I clarified that it was *their* responsibility to resolve *their* conflict. Finally, I introduced them to—and helped them work through—my **CALM** Model for conflict resolution.

SANTA'S CALM MODEL

Clarify the Issue
(Think it through yourself)

* What am I upset about? What actually happened?
* What am I feeling? Why do I feel that way?
* How might I have contributed to the problem?
* What are my long-term desired outcomes for the situation?

Address the Problem
(Share your feelings with the other person)

❋ Here's what happened…

❋ Here's how that made me feel…

❋ Here's how it negatively impacted me, my work,
and others…

Listen to the Other Side
(Understand his/her feelings)

❋ Give your total attention. Never interrupt.

❋ Ask questions (for clarification only).

❋ Focus on understanding rather than convincing.

Manage Your Way to Resolution
(Decide what you'll do)

❋ Agree that a problem exists.

❋ Identify each other's concerns and needs.

❋ Explore possible win-win solutions.

❋ Focus on what's right, **not** who's right.

❋ Agree on a course of action.

❋ Determine how missteps will be handled.

❋ Close on a positive note.

Push Pride and Professionalism

As leaders, everything we do affects and impacts those whom we lead. When we do our jobs well—with our team members' best interests paramount in our minds—we're actually providing our people with gifts: the gifts of great leadership. And when our activities are geared toward helping our employees learn, grow, and develop the work habits of success, we're giving those who rely on us gifts which will serve them well throughout their careers...gifts that last a lifetime.

Based on the feedback I have received from my reindeer and elves—including those who have left us to accept advancement positions with other major toy producers—one of the most appreciated lifetime gifts I have given my staff is a continual emphasis on **PRIDE** and **PROFESSIONALISM**. We teach those concepts, we discuss them, we expect them, we reward them, and we quickly address the infrequent times when they are found to be lacking within our operation. All of that emphasis and attention begins for each team member on their very first day when, at new-hire orientation, I share the following thoughts and beliefs:

Everything you do here at our workshop bears your personal signature. Each action you take—the way you complete every task, assignment, project, or job duty—is a reflection of **YOU.** And that fact leads to two questions everyone needs to ponder and be concerned with:

1. What does my "personal signature" look like?

2. Does it portray someone who exhibits pride in him/herself and the work they perform?

SANTA SUMMARY
GIVE THEM GIFTS THAT LAST A LIFETIME

- ☑ **Teach Success Skills**

- ☑ **Reinforce Relationships**

- ☑ **Push Pride and Professionalism**

7

GET BEYOND
THE RED WAGONS

Help Everyone Accept the Reality of Change

There's an old saying: the only constant in life and in business is **CHANGE**. And for those of us who live and work at the North Pole, nothing exemplifies that saying more than "red wagons."

It used to be that one of the most popular toys we produced and delivered were shiny red wagons. The elves made tons of them. They loved to make them; they were a happy little bunch of "wagon masters"— until the day I had to tell them that, based on the letters I was receiving, the demand for wagons was way down.

Video games were "in," and the workshop crew needed to change what they did and how they operated.

I wasn't looking forward to being the messenger on that one. As the leader, I had to make change happen with both decisiveness and sensitivity. To keep the same level of commitment they had shown to red wagons, I couldn't just dictate change, I had to orchestrate it. That involved applying several strategies—ones I've replicated many times in response to the never-ending need to move in new directions.

First, I complimented the elves on their history of red wagon excellence and expressed my pride in their past accomplishments. *Next,* I introduced the change we were facing and explained *why* it was necessary. I laid out the facts—the raw data and evidence—and asked if anyone interpreted the information differently than I did. *Then*, we discussed the benefits to be gained—individually and collectively—for making the required change. Immediately *after that*, I asked for everyone's commitment to the new direction...and got it. I reciprocated with two commitments of my own: 1) To provide the training and support that employees would need to make the changes—and feel good about themselves in the process, and 2) To demonstrate patience and understanding as they worked their way through the new learning curve. *Finally*, I made sure that everyone on the team understood that change of

this nature was inevitable—we had no choice whether or not it would come. Our only choice was how we responded to it.

How have they responded? Just see what's out there next holiday season. You'll find a lot more than red wagons…and an equal amount of smiling little faces!

Remember: the Customer Is Really in Charge

There are many catalysts for the changes we continually have to make. But unquestionably, the largest number of the changes we face and make originate from the need to respond to our customers—as with the red wagon situation.

As holiday wants and needs change, we have to change along with them. Doing so starts with accepting the fact that the customer is truly in charge of our business and then continues by setting into place plans for looking outside our snow-covered walls to make sure we have our fingers on the pulse of the market.

For us, the name of the game quickly became *field trips*…a lot more field trips than the once-a-year pilgrimage experienced only by me, a harness full of reindeer, and the couple of elves who ride shotgun.

We do *virtual* field trips—through letters, emails, telephone calls, and internet research. And we do *actual* field trips where, on a rotational basis, we send employees south, incognito. Their purpose: to meet and greet and find out what's happening with both *our* customers and our competitors...and *their* customers.

To be sure, the information we collect on our "field trips" is valuable and beneficial. But the *process* of collecting that data has proven to be even more beneficial. It's helped the elves and reindeer understand (better than any training program could convey) that everything we do revolves around customers...and that changing to meet their needs is a good thing. Now employees are actually *recommending* change instead of being "victims" of it and lamenting that the old guy in the red suit can't seem to make up his mind.

Teach "the Business" of the Business

Our experiences both with red wagons and the field trip strategy led me to an important conclusion—which has since become a key Santa leadership principle: **the more employees understand about how the business works, the more likely they are to accept and support change**.

As our team doesn't necessarily have a business background, I started by having our training group develop and conduct a basic business literacy course through which everyone would learn concepts like "cash flow" and "cost of goods sold" (or in our case, cost of goods *delivered*).

I then "opened up the books"—giving the staff more access to financial information such as production costs, overhead expenses, and the like. And we gave that information true meaning by teaching the elves and reindeer how to read and interpret the data and how to *use* it in the performance of their jobs.

That was followed by instituting regular **State of the Workshop** meetings to keep everyone informed about what's happening (future plans, new products, planned purchases and upgrades, staffing issues, field trip reports, etc.).

A series of brainstorming exercises led to three other highly successful initiatives:

Having different elves and reindeer attend, observe, and even participate in nonconfidential senior-staff meetings.

 Cross-training and rotating assignments within departments so employees can understand and appreciate the functions of, and challenges faced by, their coworkers.

 A departmental "swap" program that allows individuals to experience how other business units operate and how we're all interdependent in achieving our overall mission.

For us, teaching "the business" of the business has been *good business*. It's given the elves and reindeer additional opportunities to get involved in what we do, it's helped them grow and develop, and it's produced greater workshop-wide acceptance, support, and understanding of the need for change.

Most importantly, it's made them feel like true "partners" in the running of our North Pole operation… because **THEY ARE!**

SANTA SUMMARY:
GET BEYOND THE RED WAGONS

✓ **Help Everyone Accept the Reality of Change**

✓ **Remember: the Customer Is Really in Charge**

✓ **Teach "the Business" of the Business**

8

SHARE THE MILK AND COOKIES

Help Them See the Difference They Make

Although everyone on our team works diligently to make sure our mission is accomplished, *I'm* the one in the spotlight. Who are the zillions of letters we receive each year addressed to? Me. Who gets the credit for the elf-made presents found under all those trees each year? Me. Who enjoys milk and freshly baked cookies in warm homes while the reindeer try to catch their breath on cold rooftops? Me again. And who is the only member of our North Pole team who regularly gets to get out and see, firsthand, the smiles that our

work produces? Yep, you guessed it…it's me.

Those benefits (and many more like them) are a large part of what gets and keeps me motivated. They're great—great, that is, if you happen to be *me*. But, unfortunately, there's only one Santa. And, with the exception of an occasional field trip, most of the elves and reindeer don't get to see and experience the same things that I do. So their feelings of satisfaction and accomplishment must come in different ways—from their leader.

A key strategy I apply in performing that role is to help each elf and reindeer see the positive differences that he or she is making for those we serve… and for each other; I help them see *their* part of the big "making-people-happy" picture.

I start out by spending time with all members of the workshop team discussing how their functions, efforts, and contributions are vital to what we do. Doing so reinforces two messages that I'm constantly communicating to the staff: 1) We don't make and deliver toys, we make and deliver *happiness*, and 2) We couldn't do that without **YOU!**

I make it a priority to spend one-on-one time with each and every elf and reindeer—telling them face-to-face how their individual talents contribute to the team and make a difference to those who will unwrap their handiwork on Christmas morning.

I also make sure that everyone sees the scores of thank-you letters that start coming in around mid-January. I post them on a large board in the workshop that's labeled: **SEE WHAT YOU MADE HAPPEN.** I also post my reply (thank you for the thank you) letters—which always begin with the words, "On behalf of all the elves and reindeer…" And I often ask members of the staff to write and sign the replies themselves.

Finally, I take a few elves with me on each season's delivery run. When we return, I call a full-team meeting at which my traveling companions and I share our experiences with everyone.

Nothing motivates employees more than knowing they're making a difference. Find ways to make that happen in *your* workshop.

Do Right by Those Who Do Right

I admit it. There was a period, long ago, when I had fallen into the trap of taking my workers for granted. Things were running smoothly. So I regularly responded to the team's achievements with **NO RESPONSE.** I said and did nothing as long as my expectations were being met.

Then one afternoon, as we were loading the sleigh for our big run, one of the elves asked a very profound question. "Hey, Boss," he said. "Good little girls and boys get all these toys. What do good elves and reindeer get?"

I thought about those words all Eve long. By the time we returned to the North Pole, I realized that I had failed to apply one of the basic premises of our

business to my employees: good performance should be reinforced with positive consequences.

Since that experience, I've worked hard at developing one of the most important characteristics of effective leadership: an "attitude of gratitude." I've learned to truly appreciate workers who meet or exceed my expectations. More importantly, I've learned to *show* that appreciation through my actions and behaviors. I look for, and seize, opportunities to give verbal and written atta-elves (and atta-deers)—opportunities to say *thank you* for doing right.

I've learned that recognizing employees—doing right by those who do right—is one of the best things I can do for my elves and reindeer—and for myself as well. *I* feel good when I do it, *they* feel good when they receive it, and they're more motivated, therefore more likely to repeat the performance I want and need in the future.

Everyone wins. What a deal. It's happy holidays for all!

Expand the Reinforcement Possibilities

Now I operate by a simple rule of thumb: the more reinforcement of good work, the merrier. But that's not necessarily an easy rule to live by. Why? Because of two misconceptions common in workshops across the land:

1. **"There's very little we can do. Money and options are limited."**

2. **"Recognition and reinforcement are strictly management activities, and we only have so many managers."**

We tackled the first misconception with thought and creativity. I worked on my own, and then with my team leaders, to develop a list of low-cost, high-impact ways to recognize our elves and reindeer. We challenged ourselves to come up with as many ideas as possible. From letters home to families, to special training and assignments—from prime spots in the employee sleigh lot, to appreciation certificates we printed in the shop—from nominations for our formal awards program, to springing for (you knew it was coming) milk and cookies—the possibilities were and are endless!

Addressing the second misconception—that reinforcing and recognizing good work was management's job alone—proved to be a horse (make that reindeer) of a different color...and a bit more challenging. The task was to get workshop-wide acceptance of the notion that recognition was everyone's job...*everyone's* responsibility. And that meant changing some long-held beliefs and accompanying behaviors.

I started with real workshop examples to help everyone see how we **ALL** benefit from the good work of individual elves, reindeer, and team leaders. Then I asked for a show of hands and hooves of those who regularly praised their coworkers. As expected, the count was very small. When I asked why that was, the most common response was, "That's your job, not ours." I responded with, "Why is that? Why shouldn't everyone be grateful...and show it?" No one had a good answer.

I immediately asked them all to give it a try, and they agreed. I made and distributed a sheet listing ways to recognize and reinforce coworker performance. And

I've kept the concept alive by talking about it at staff meetings, doing it myself, and by making sure I give recognition to those who recognize others.

Look for ways to expand the reinforcement possibilities where you work. Make that previously mentioned "attitude of gratitude" one of *your* most important workshop values.

SANTA SUMMARY:
SHARE THE MILK AND COOKIES

✓ **Help Them See the Difference They Make**

✓ **Do Right by Those Who Do Right**

✓ **Expand the Reinforcement Possibilities**

FIND OUT WHO'S NAUGHTY AND NICE

Confront Performance Problems Early

Igor was one of the original elves here at the Pole when we started this business. I was new to the job—anxious to make my mark on the world, expecting each employee to be nice so I too could be nothing but nice and well-liked. When he started, Igor was just that—nice. But things slowly began to change. I noticed that Igor would occasionally start his shift a few minutes late and take longer-than-scheduled breaks and lunches. My response was **NO** response—which I rationalized with "I'll let it slide because he does good work". So

I overlooked Igor's tardiness (Mistake No. 1)—hoping that it would magically go away on its own. Of course, it didn't...it continued.

Then, instead of dealing with Igor one-on-one, I chose to send out a memo to the entire workshop staff reminding everyone of the importance of being on time (Mistake No. 2). I hoped Igor would read it, get the message, and correct the problem without my involvement. Of course, he didn't. And all the other elves were left wondering why I sent a reminder about something they already knew and were abiding by.

As the problem continued, I looked for every excuse to avoid a confrontation (Mistake No. 3). But the issue came to a head when one of the other elves approached me and asked, "When are you gonna do something about Igor? His being late all the time is really unfair to the rest of us." I knew I had to do something, and I was furious that Igor had put me in this position. So I called him into my office and unloaded on him (Mistake No. 4).

We were both angry and the tension was high. And then *he* asked a question that shut me up faster than a raised eyebrow from Mrs. Claus: "If this issue is so important, why didn't you say something to me sooner?" There was no good answer to offer, only excuses—the same type of excuses I wouldn't accept from others. I *had* been unfair to the other elves…and to Igor as well. I'd seen something I didn't like—something I knew was wrong—and I had failed to do anything about it. I was as much to blame for Igor's continuing problem as he was…and I knew it. I swore, then and there, never to let that happen again. And I haven't. Now I deal with performance problems early and calmly—before they get **BIG**.

Coach the Majority in the Middle

What do you think about when you gaze at the sky on a clear night? What do you see? I see stars…lots of them. And those stars remind me of my elves and reindeer. There are **falling stars** that represent the few employees who exhibit performance problems like Igor, and there are bright novas—the **superstars** that represent the opposite in employee performance. However, most of the lights in the sky are neither falling stars nor supernovas. They're what I call the **middle stars**, and they typify the vast majority of all employees.

The middle star group is the backbone of our

workshop. They're the good, solid workers who, day in, day out, bring our mission to life. And many of them have either positive or negative potential; some have the capacity to experience superstardom, while others run the risk of slipping into the falling-star ranks.

Obviously, for us to be successful, it's imperative that these middle stars avoid falling backwards. They need to continue on as good performers or, better yet, move to the superior-performer level. And as a leader, I play *the* critical role in making that happen. I meet that responsibility by applying various strategies

and techniques that fall within the broad management category known as "coaching." As the older I get the simpler I like things, and I've come to define coaching very simply: helping the elves and reindeer avoid problems and do the best work that they can. And doing that with my middle stars includes the following:

 Making sure that they know and understand the performance expectations that come with employment.

 Providing the training and resources they need to meet those expectations.

 Giving frequent and specific feedback on how they're doing.

 Identifying any obstacles they may be facing and then doing my best to eliminate those barriers.

Teaching them how to set, manage, and achieve goals.

 Helping them learn from mistakes and successes.

 Partnering with mentors from the superstar ranks.

and, as I learned from the Igor experience…

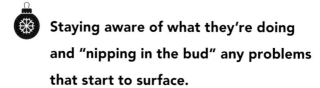 **Staying aware of what they're doing and "nipping in the bud" any problems that start to surface.**

When it comes to managing the majority in the middle, the goal is clear: make sure they avoid being naughty, help them stay nice, and work with them to get even "nicer"!

Don't Forget the Superstars

Bet you didn't know that I'm a huge sports fan. It's true! I love sporting events of all kinds, and I watch them on television every chance I get. I especially enjoy championship games and the Olympics because they involve "the best of the best" athletes—many of whom started in their sport with equipment from us!

Each time I watch, I notice a very interesting fact: before, during, and after their events, superstars spend time talking with—and listening to—their coaches. They **ALL** have coaches…and they often credit current and past coaches for helping them become the superior performers that they are. After all, people don't get to the top of anything all by themselves. And few, if any, *stay* on top without help and guidance from others. That's the essence of coaching…and the essence of this next leadership gift for you.

Your superstars earned their way into that category just like my top elves and reindeer did—by exhibiting

consistently outstanding performance. And I used to think that the best thing I could do for those folks was to leave them alone and let them do *their* thing. Boy was I wrong! Like everyone else, great performers don't like to be ignored or taken for granted. Even though some may not admit it publicly, in private most realize that they need to be worked with, involved, recognized, and rewarded. In other words, they need to be coached. But with this group, the coaching role is a little different. For me, it's one of Santa the Encourager, Santa the Developer, and Santa the Cheerleader. And just like with the middle stars, I have several specific techniques I employ. I make a special effort to:

 Get them involved in decision-making, strategy setting, procedure development, and problem solving.

 Encourage them to teach and mentor others...including me.

 Provide them with highly specialized training and other career-growth opportunities.

 Avoid punishing them for good performance. ("You did such a good job handling that mess, the next time we get one, we'll give it to you again.")

As a leader, the key to dealing with superstars is to demonstrate—through words and actions—that you know and appreciate the fact that they are the *nicest* of "the nice."

SANTA SUMMARY:
FIND OUT WHO'S NAUGHTY AND NICE

☑ **Confront Performance Problems Early**

☑ **Coach the Majority in the Middle**

☑ **Don't Forget the Superstars**

10

BE GOOD FOR
GOODNESS SAKE

Set the Example

Imagine what would happen if we had just one ethics slip at the North Pole...just one time when we failed to do the right thing. It would be disastrous. Our excellent reputation—built over centuries of hard work and attention to detail—could be tarnished (or destroyed entirely) by a single inappropriate act.

How could the customers we serve ever believe in a Santa and crew who broke the rules, cut corners, or failed to meet their commitments?

The answer is: they couldn't! And that would quickly spell the end of our legend...and our business. That's

why ethics is so important to us—that's why making sure that integrity "happens" is one of my most critical responsibilities.

You see, I'm the leader here. And obviously, I have a strong influence on the thoughts and behaviors of the elves and the reindeer. They rightfully assume that it's okay to do whatever *I* do. Regardless of what's said or written elsewhere in the workshop, my actions— whether good or bad—are the performance standards that they will follow.

There's no getting around it: I must model the behaviors that I expect from others. I must take the **LEAD**. I must be the first to "walk the talk" when it comes to things like:

 Following ALL of our rules and procedures.

 Treating EVERYONE with dignity and respect.

 ALWAYS telling the truth.

 NEVER breaking a promise or commitment.

 Building superior quality into EVERYTHING I do.

 CONTINUALLY giving my best effort.

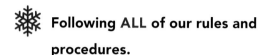 **CONSISTENTLY taking a stand for what's right.**

Would you expect anything less from Santa Claus? Probably not. My workers expect nothing less of me either. And *your* people expect the same of **YOU!**

Establish Guidelines and Accountability

Because ethics is so important to us, I can't rely on my example alone for ensuring that everyone does the right thing. Certainly I do my best to bring on workers who value and demonstrate integrity. But no one is perfect, so reminders need to be made!

I make sure that all staff members are well-versed in the laws, rules, and procedures that apply to them. We spend a lot of time discussing—in specific, "how to" terms—what it means to be ethical. And, to help guide their (and my) actions and decisions, we worked together to develop this:

THE WORKSHOP
"WHAT'S RIGHT?" TEST

 1. Is it legal?

 2. Does it comply with our workshop rules and guidelines?

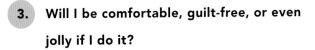 **3.** Will I be comfortable, guilt-free, or even jolly if I do it?

 **4.** Does it support our goals, commitments, and mission?

 5. Would I be perfectly okay with someone doing it to me?

 6. Would the most ethical individual I know of do it?

All the guidelines we provide are valuable and important. But for them to have true meaning and really matter, they must be backed with accountabilities and consequences. Just as most children know that being naughty can result in Santa skipping their house, everyone here at the workshop knows that doing wrong will likely result in a coaching session from Santa…or worse.

For me, building accountability for proper behavior involves the following:

 Keeping my eyes and ears open to what's happening.

 Providing ongoing feedback.

 Displaying zero tolerance.

Think the elves might resent this level of accountability? Well, they don't. They actually support it. Some even demand it. They expect me to take a strong stand in preserving the principles that they take so much pride in having.

Remember That Everything Counts

It was a Friday afternoon. After about twenty little ones came and went, Michael took his turn on my knee. "Well, Michael," I asked, "have you been a good little boy?" "Yes, I have," he replied. And then he continued, "I've been very good. Maybe I did tell a little lie. And I cheated on a game and called my sister stupid. But those things don't count...do they, Santa?"

"Actually, Michael, those things *do* count," I replied. "Being good means being good all the time. There are no time-outs...no crossing your fingers behind your back. *Everything* counts."

When it comes to our business, we've never broken any laws (at least none that I know about) or fibbed about our finances. I'm guessing that your workshop can make the same claim. Most can. But doing right involves a lot more than avoiding those big "corporate sins." I've learned that it's our day-in, day-out, seemingly insignificant actions and behaviors that determine our overall goodness. I constantly remind myself of that as I work to set the proper example and hold everyone accountable. Everything counts toward our big goals at the end of the year!

Here at the workshop, we *do* focus on the big integrity issues. But we also give equal, if not more, attention to the "small stuff." I challenge myself and my staff to periodically examine just how ethical we are by looking at:

 The way we treat and talk about each other.

 The little white lies we don't (or do) tell.

 The commitments we make and keep (or don't keep).

 The workshop supplies we don't (or do) take home.

The "unimportant" rules we follow (or break).

The level of quality we put into our toys.

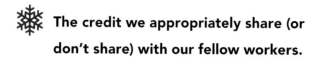 **The credit we appropriately share (or don't share) with our fellow workers.**

EVERYTHING COUNTS—for your people and especially for *you* as their leader.

SANTA SUMMARY:
BE GOOD FOR GOODNESS SAKE

✓ **Set the Example**

✓ **Establish Guidelines and Accountability**

✓ **Remember That Everything Counts**

CLOSING THOUGHTS

There's a question that has been pondered for centuries and probably will be debated for years to come:

Is Santa Claus a real person?

Well, *I* think I am. The elves and reindeer think so too. Mrs. Claus certainly believes I exist. But truth be told, whether or not I'm "real" isn't all that important. There are, however, two facts that are *very* important… and very real:

1. **To survive and prosper, you and your organization must be able to achieve "big things" throughout each year.**

2. **You can't get those big things done without effective leadership.**

You see, **it's not easy being a leader**. Your job comes with many challenges and responsibilities, as you well know. But it is an important and necessary job. And

it can be a rewarding one—if you do it right. Helping you do that is precisely what *The Leadership Secrets of Santa Claus* is all about.

With this book, you've been given a valuable gift wrapped in a bunch of good wishes. What you choose to do with it, however, is entirely up to you. There's no question that *your* elves and reindeer are depending on you—just as you depend on them. Don't let them down! Apply the concepts and strategies you've been exposed to within these pages. Take advantage of other resources and opportunities to hone your personal skills. Those are the greatest gifts *you* can give to your people, your organization, and yourself.

Most importantly, never forget that getting big things done all year long isn't about magic. It's about leadership.

Happy holidays. Happy all days!

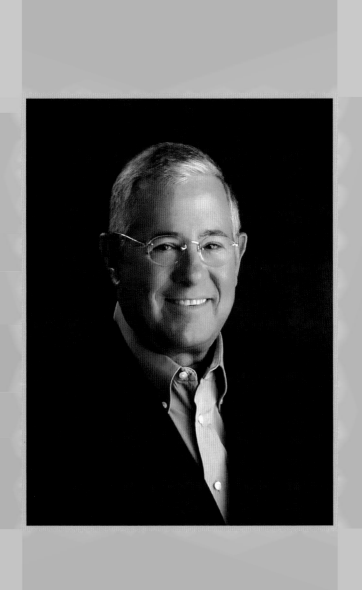

ABOUT THE AUTHOR

Eric Harvey is founder and president of the Walk the Talk Company and a leading expert on high-achieving leaders and organizations. Since its founding in 1977, Walk the Talk has worked with thousands of organizations worldwide, including multinational corporations, leading healthcare providers, high-tech start-ups, and highly respected nonprofit organizations. Eric has authored twenty-five books that have sold millions of copies, including the bestsellers *Walk the Talk, Ethics 4 Everyone, Walk Awhile in My Shoes*, and *Go for the Gold*. He and his wife, Nancy, live in Pensacola Beach, Florida, and are the proud parents of two daughters and six grandchildren.